ECOCRAFTS

Creative
Costumes

KINGFISHER

KINGFISHER

Kingfisher Publications Plc
New Penderel House
283-288 High Holborn
London WC1V 7HZ
www.kingfisherpub.com

First published by Kingfisher Publications Plc 2007
10 9 8 7 6 5 4 3 2 1
1TR/0507/C&C/MAR(MAR)/128OJIEX-GREEN/C

Authors: Dawn Brend, Kirsty Neale,
Cheryl Owen, Melanie Williams

For Toucan
Editor: Theresa Bebbington
Designer: Leah Germann
Photography Art Direction: Jane Thomas
Photographer: Andy Crawford
Editorial Director: Ellen Dupont

For Kingfisher
Senior Editor: Catherine Brereton
Art Director: Mike Davis
Senior Production Controller: Lindsey Scott
DTP Coordinator: Catherine Hibbert

A CIP catalogue record for this book is available
from the British Library.

ISBN 978 07534 1481 1

Printed in China

**The paper used for the cover and text pages is
made from 100% recycled post-consumer waste.**

ECOCRAFTS

Creative Costumes

Contents

Eco-wise

It might be hard to decide which is more fun: making your own costumes or wearing them. By creating your own costumes, you make sure they will be special to you – no one else will have costumes that are exactly the same as yours.

As well as being really special, all the projects in this book help the environment by using everyday things found in your home. A lot of them are items you would have thrown away. You'll find ways to use card and newspaper to make a monster mask, use coat hangers to create wings for a fairy, turn plastic bags into a wizard's cape and even reuse a big T-shirt to make a witch's dress. Recycling helps the planet because it reuses things that would have ended up in the dustbin.

Around the world tonnes of rubbish ends up in landfills each year. In the UK alone, we

3 'R's to recycling

About half of the rubbish in our dustbins can be recycled. Follow these steps to help prevent rubbish being sent to landfills or incinerators.

REDUCE – Encourage your parents to buy products that have little or no packaging.
REUSE – Find new ways to use jars, tins, plastic containers and other durable things.
RECYCLE – If you can't reuse something but it can be recycled, help your parents recycle it.

dump 28 million tonnes of household rubbish into landfills every year. This rubbish weighs the same amount as three-and-a-half million double-decker buses. If you lined up all these buses, they would wrap around Earth two-and-a-half times. Each year we create more rubbish than the year before, and if we continue to do so, it's thought that we'll double the amount of rubbish we produce by 2020.

When we throw away so much rubbish, we are also throwing away valuable resources. If we recycle our rubbish, fewer materials will need to be mined, quarried or grown, and less energy is used to transport these materials around the world. Another concern is that the landfills where rubbish is buried are filling up – and there's little space left to make new landfills.

What you can do

Grown out of your clothes? If they are in good condition, give them to a younger brother or sister. Or donate old clothes to a charity shop, which can sell them to someone who they will fit.

If your old clothes are too stained or are ripped, use the good pieces of fabric to make something else. You can even sew pieces together to make a small blanket for a favourite doll.

If you've been given old clothes, see what's in fashion in the shops and think about how you can change them. Perhaps sew on some buttons in a pattern.

If a room is being redecorated, ask if you can save any old curtains, tablecloths or even cushion covers to reuse the fabric to make something else.

Getting started

Before starting a project, make sure you have everything you need. You may have to trace a picture or do some sewing. If you're not sure how to do these things, follow the steps here. Some craft supplies are not meant for children under 13 to use. If you're not sure if something is safe for you to use, ask an adult if it's okay. When using craft supplies that have a strong odour, work in a room that has plenty of fresh air. If an object is difficult to cut, ask an adult to help.

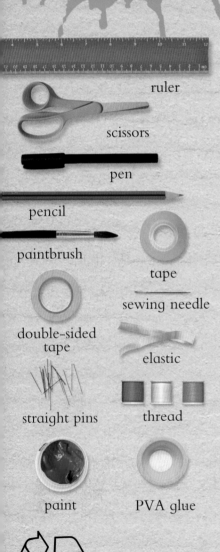

ruler

scissors

pen

pencil

paintbrush

tape

sewing needle

double-sided tape

elastic

straight pins

thread

paint

PVA glue

Sewing Tips

Be careful when you handle sewing needles and straight pins, which are sharp and can prick.

To thread a needle, cut the end of the thread at an angle and wet it with saliva. It will be easier to fit it through the eye of a needle.

To make a knot at the end of the thread, wrap it around your forefinger a few times, roll it off between your finger and thumb, and pull it tight.

For a finishing knot, make a tiny stitch into the fabric, wrap the thread around the needle and pull the needle. Cut off the extra thread.

MAKING A SQUARE KNOT

You can use this knot to tie the ends of elastic together. Once you tie the knot, trim off the ends.

STEP 1

Make a simple overhand knot by bringing the ends together and feeding the left end over the right.

STEP 2

Make another overhand knot in the opposite direction, with the right end over the left end.

TYPES OF STITCHES

When making stitches, keep the spaces and stitch sizes as even as you can. The running stitch is a simple stitch to hold two seams together. If you want a really strong seam, you can use the backstitch in steps 1 and 2 for all the stitches. To gather material, skip steps 1 and 2, and let the knot in the thread hold it in place. Then make tacking stitches – these are simply large running stitches, but they are about 2 to 3 centimetres long.

STEP 1

Make a backstitch by inserting the needle up through the fabric, then down behind where the thread exits the fabric, 5 millimetres behind it.

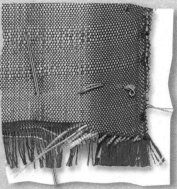

STEP 2

Now bring the needle up again, 5 millimetres in front of the thread. This secures the end of the thread. Now make the running stitches in step 3.

STEP 3

Pass the needle over and under the fabric, along the seam, making a few stitches at a time, then pulling the thread. At the end use a finishing knot (see Sewing Tips, left).

TRACING A PICTURE

If you have a pencil, pen, tracing paper and tape, you can copy any picture you want. The pencil should have soft lead – this will make it easier to do the rubbing over the back. Use a pen with a hard point to make the lines really crisp.

STEP 1

Tape down a sheet of tracing paper over the picture you wish to draw. Using a pen with a hard point, copy the picture onto the tracing paper.

STEP 2

Remove the tracing paper from the picture. Rub a soft-lead pencil on the back of the tracing paper where you can see the lines you have drawn.

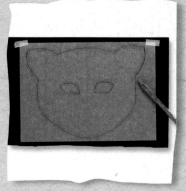

STEP 3

Tape the tracing paper where you want the picture, with the pencil-side facing down. Draw over the lines with a pen. Remove the paper.

Scales and tail

Pastel-coloured plastic bags will make brilliant scales for a fantastic mermaid costume. Decorate an old top and make your own special headband, and your mermaid outfit will make you a real queen of the sea!

YOU WILL NEED:
....
bin liner, plastic bags, scissors, double-sided tape, ruler, card, pencil, old vest, PVA glue, paintbrush, elastic, paint, wrapping paper, ribbon (for wrapping gifts), glitter

ECOFACT
Reusing one tonne of plastic bags saves about 11 barrels of oil, which is used to make plastic. In New York City alone, if each person used one fewer plastic bag in a year, waste would be reduced by more than 2,000 tonnes that year.

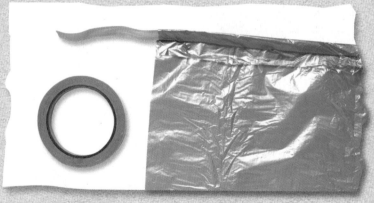

STEP 1

To make the skirt, cut a bin liner so it is long enough to reach your ankles and is 20 centimetres wider than your waist. Cut a curved shape at the bottom.

STEP 2

Place a strip of double-sided tape 3 centimetres from the top of the skirt. Cut a piece of elastic a little longer than your waist. Lay it above the tape, fold over the edge of the skirt and press it into the tape – don't let the elastic disappear into the seam. Tie the elastic ends into a knot.

STEP 3

To join the two front edges of the skirt together, lay the skirt flat on the ground, with the opening on top. Lift up one side of the skirt and stick double-sided tape down the straight edge of the other side (stop before it curves). Push the first side down on the tape.

STEP 4

Choose plastic bags in different colours, such as pink and blue, and cut scale shapes from them. Also cut some strips of plastic, about 10 to 15 centimetres long, from extra pieces of the bin liner.

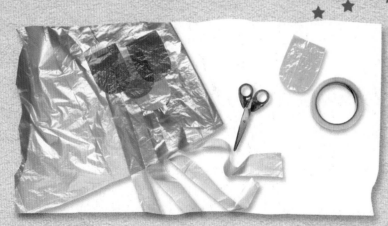

STEP 5

Decorate the skirt by sticking the scales and strips to it. First tape the strips around the bottom of the skirt. Then beginning at the bottom, tape a row of scales around the skirt.

STEP 6

Continue sticking the scales onto the skirt, making sure each new row of scales overlaps the row of scales below it. Once you've finished taping on the scales, choose a few scales and glue some glitter on them.

Scales and tail

STEP 7

For the top, cut out a pair of scallop-shaped shells from a blue plastic bag.

STEP 8

Brush glue along the lines on the shells. Sprinkle glitter over the glue and allow the glue to dry.

STEP 9

Splatter some paint on an old, light-coloured vest, or ask an adult to spray some paint on it.

STEP 10

Using double-sided tape, attach the shells to the top in a bikini-like style.

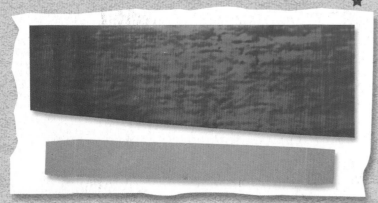

STEP 11

For the headband, cut a piece of card so it fits halfway around your head and is 4 centimetres wide. Cut some wrapping paper large enough to cover the band.

STEP 12

Brush some glue onto the card and wrap the paper around it – make sure the paper lies flat and smooth. Allow the glue to dry. For a neat look, cut a curved shape at each end.

STEP 13

Cut a piece of elastic a few centimetres longer than the headband. Poke a hole in each end of the band. Feed one end of the elastic into each hole and tie a knot.

STEP 14

Cut some long strips of wrapping paper and ribbon. Beginning at one end, where the card meets the elastic, tape alternating lengths of ribbon and wrapping paper.

STEP 15

Continue taping the strips around the band until you reach the other end of the elastic. Finally, curl the strips by running a ruler sharply along them.

Wear the headband with the strips in front and pretend they are mermaid hair.

Make a really big splash when you put on this great mermaid outfit.

13

A fairy-tale fairy

You can turn an old vest and lacy tablecloth or curtain into a beautiful fairy dress. Add your own special wings and a wand, and you'll soon have a magical costume. A pink vest and pink plastic bags will make the best outfit. Be careful when handling the pins.

YOU WILL NEED:
....

old vest, pen, lace tablecloth or curtains, ruler or tape measure, scissors, straight pins, thread, sewing needle, gems, PVA glue, paintbrush, two clothes hangers, tape, plastic bags, elastic, card, plant cane, paint, ribbon, sequins

STEP 1

To make the dress, put on your vest and mark with a pen where it sits at your waist. Take off the vest, and at the mark draw a line around the vest.

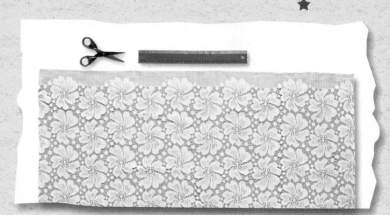

STEP 2

To make the skirt section of the dress, cut the lace tablecloth or cutains into four rectanglar panels, each one about 50 x 70 centimetres.

STEP 3

For each panel, fold it over diagonally, so two corners form triangles at the bottom (as shown here). The middle section of the fold will be attached to the dress.

STEP 4

Make pleats along the middle section of the fold by overlapping the fabric every 2 to 3 centimetres and holding each pleat in place with a straight pin.

A floral pattern makes pretty lacy panels, but you can use any pattern you like.

STEP 5

Pin one panel to the front of the vest, along the line at the waist, one panel to the back, and one panel to each side. Sew them on using a running stitch (see page 9), passing the needle through all the layers of fabric. Or ask an adult to sew them on for you. Remove the pins.

STEP 6

Decorate the vest by adding gems or sequins onto it, making a border along the top and a heart in the centre. You can use self-stick gems or glue them in place. If you wish, you can also glue on some flower decorations.

A fairy-tale fairy

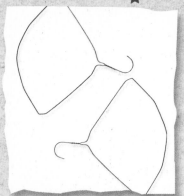

STEP 7

For the wings, bend out the bottom of two metal clothes hangers, so they form a wing-like shape.

STEP 8

Ask an adult to twist the two hooked ends together. Wrap tape around the hooks to secure them.

STEP 9

Place a plastic bag over a hanger, wrap the top end around the hook section and tape it in place.

STEP 10

Repeat for the second wing, wrapping the end neatly around the hook section for a nice finish.

STEP 11

Cut two pieces of elastic long enough to loop around your arms. Tape them to the wings.

STEP 12

For the wand, draw a star on some card (a cereal box is ideal) and cut it out. Use the star as a template to make a second star of exactly the same size.

STEP 13

Ask an adult to cut a garden cane so it is 45 centimetres long. Paint the stars and the cane. Leave them to dry.

16

STEP 14

Wind some ribbon around the cane and tape the ends down. Tape a star to the top of the cane, then tape thin pieces of ribbon to the back of the star.

STEP 15

Glue the second star to the back of the first star and decorate the star by gluing on some sequins.

You'll feel like a real fairy wearing these wings and dress. To make them extra special, glue some sequins to the skirt and add glitter glue to the wings.

Princess for a day

The cape and tiara will make this princess dress a dream that has come true. Making this outfit is a great way to reuse old fabrics. When choosing the fabric for the skirt, make sure there is enough for the sleeves, too.

YOU WILL NEED:

fabric for the skirt and sleeves, tape measure, chalk, scissors, sewing needle, thread, short-sleeved top, straight pins, sequins, gems, PVA glue, paintbrush, net curtain, two safety pins, elastic, heavy fabric, curtain tie rope, trimming (from an old curtain or cushion), card, headband, paint, tape, pink fabric

STEP 1

For the sleeves, cut two semi-circles from the fabric for the skirt. Make tacking stitches (see page 9) along the straight edge of each sleeve.

STEP 2

For each sleeve, pull the thread to gather the fabric, making sure it fits on the short-sleeved top. Use straight pins to hold the sleeve in place on the top. Sew the sleeve to the top using a running stitch (see page 9).

18

STEP 3

Dab some glue onto the back of some sequins and gems and stick them around the neckline on the top. Choose your favourite gem to use at the centre of the neckline.

STEP 4

Cut a piece of fabric long enough for a knee-length skirt and 30 centimetres wider than your waist. Cut a net curtain the same width, but to reach your ankles.

Pin an end of the elastic to the fabric so it doesn't slip into the hem as you work.

STEP 5

Fold over the top 5 centimetres of the net fabric and sew along it to make a hem. Attach a safety pin to one end of a piece of elastic 10 centimetres longer than your waist. Push the pin through the hem to feed the elastic into it. Tie the ends into a knot. Repeat for the skirt.

STEP 6

For the cloak, cut a piece of fabric big enough to drape over your shoulders and to reach below your knees. Sew a hem in the top as in step 5, but feed a curtain tie rope through it. Glue some trimming to the bottom. Leave to dry.

19

Princess for a day

STEP 7

For the tiara, use a headband to trace the bottom edge on card, draw a tab, then draw the top curvy edge, as shown here. Cut out the card.

STEP 8

Paint the card silver on one side. Once dry, paint the other side of the tiara. Leave to dry.

STEP 9

Fit the tiara card around the headband and fold over the tab. Tape the tab firmly onto the headband.

STEP 10

Choose some sequins and gems that match those used on the dress, dab some glue on the back and use them to decorate the tiara. Leave to dry.

When you're ready to be princess for a day, put on your dress, tie the sash around it and make a lovely bow in the back. Now you're ready for your cloak and tiara.

STEP 11

For the sash, fold a piece of fabric 20 centimetres x 110 centimetres in half lengthwise, with the good sides that you want to see pressed together. Sew the long edge with a running stitch (see page 9). Turn it inside out and sew the short ends together.

STEP 12

For a flower, fold a piece of fabric 10 centimetres x 20 centimetres in half lengthwise, with the sides you don't want to see together. Sew the long edge with a tacking stitch (see page 9). Gather the fabric into a circle. Sew the short ends together.

STEP 13

Glue a gem to the centre of the flower and leave to dry. Once dry, sew the flower to the centre of the sash.

Wicked witch

All witches need a pointy hat, and this one is a real star. Wear it with the wicked witch's dress, made from an old black T-shirt (man's size).

YOU WILL NEED:

card, ruler, pencil, scissors, tape measure, PVA glue, paintbrush, paint, wool, star-shaped stickers, large black T-shirt, dress that fits you, paper or newspaper, straight pins, sewing needle, thread

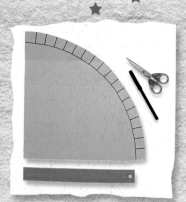

STEP 1

Draw a quarter-circle on card, with the straight sides 38 centimetres long. Cut out the shape. Draw lines along the curved edge, as shown, then cut slits along the lines.

STEP 2

For the brim, draw a circle with a 35 centimetre diameter (the distance across the centre) on card. Draw an oval shape in the centre that will fit your head. Cut out the circles.

STEP 3

Roll up the hat into a cone shape and tape the edges together. Bend out the tabs cut into the end of the cone and glue the brim to the tabs. Paint the hat black. Leave to dry.

STEP 4

To make witch's hair, cut some lengths of wool and glue them inside the back of the hat. Stick some star stickers around the hat.

STEP 5

Trace around a dress that fits you onto paper or newspaper, and cut out the shape. Use straight pins to pin the paper dress to a black T-shirt turned inside out – make sure the necklines match up.

STEP 6

Trace around the dress with a piece of chalk. Remove the straight pins and the paper dress. Cut out the shape of the dress. (You might want to use straight pins to hold the seams together.)

STEP 7

Using a running stitch (see page 9), sew along the seams up the sides of the dress and under the arms.

STEP 8

Turn the dress right-side out. Using scissors, cut a jagged fringe along the bottom edge.

Even wicked witches can have fun, so try wearing this outfit with some bright stripy tights, a nose from a joke shop and go for a ride on a witch's broomstick!

Purr-fect black cat

With some card, socks and a few other things, you'll soon be going on the prowl as the top cat in your house. Our cat is black, but you can use orange items for a ginger cat.

YOU WILL NEED:
....
black and white card, thick black pen, PVA glue, paintbrush, pink button, hat elastic, pink felt, three pairs of knee-high socks, 1-centimetre-wide black elastic

STEP 1

To trace a mask from black card (see page 9) and a muzzle from white card, use the templates on page 46. Cut them out.

STEP 2

Draw the mouth and whiskers on the muzzle with a thick black pen.

STEP 3

Spread some glue on the back of the muzzle. Place the muzzle on the mask.

STEP 4

For the nose, stick a pink button to the muzzle with PVA glue. Allow the glue to dry.

STEP 5

Ask an adult to poke a hole at each side of the mask. Thread hat elastic through the holes and make knots in the ends.

STEP 6

Cut four sets of paw pads from pink felt. Glue each set to the toe end of a black sock with PVA glue.

STEP 7

For the tail, turn a sock inside out and sew along the centre (or ask an adult to sew the sock). Turn the tail right-side out.

STEP 8

Tie the black elastic around your waist and knot the ends together. Cut off the extra elastic. Slip off the elastic and sew the top of the sock at the knot.

You can paint card from a cereal box to get the right coloured card.

For the complete look, slip the tail around your waist, put the socks over your hands and feet, and put on the mask. Now all you need to do is practise your miaows!

25

A wise wizard

For the best-looking wizard, collect plastic bags that are black, silver and gold. Along with some card from a cereal box and a few other things, these bags can be turned into a great wizard costume.

YOU WILL NEED:

plastic bags, scissors, double-sided tape, ruler, card, pencil, paint, glitter, PVA glue, paintbrush, elastic, string, white tissue paper

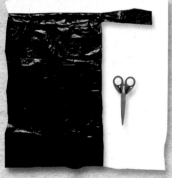

STEP 1

To make the cape, cut out a rectangle from a black plastic bag that's big enough to use as a cape. Cut a strip to use as a tie.

STEP 2

Place a strip of double-sided tape 3 centimetres from the top of the cape. Lay the plastic strip above it, then fold over the top edge of the cape, pressing it into the tape.

STEP 3

Make cuts about every 5 centimetres up the length of the cape, stopping a little before you reach the top of the cape. Try to keep the cuts straight and even.

STEP 4

Choose plastic bags in wizardy colours, such as silver and gold. Cut them into strips 5 centimetres wide. Tape the strips to the inside of your cape along the top edge.

STEP 5

To make a hat, draw a cone shape onto a large piece of card. First use some string to measure around your head. The distance between the two corners at the bottom of the cone should be a few centimetres longer than the length of the string. Cut out the shape.

STEP 6

Stick double-sided tape along a straight edge, roll the hat up and press the other edge into the tape. Paint the hat black. When dry, add glitter to the rim and paint on some stars.

STEP 7

To make a beard, draw a pair of lips onto card and cut them out. Poke a hole in each end with a pencil. Cut a piece of elastic that will fit around your head, insert each end into a hole and tie a square knot.

STEP 8

Rip some white tissue paper into three beard shapes, each one slighter larger than the previous one. Layer them, with the largest on bottom and smallest on top, and glue together. Glue on the mouth. When dry, cut out a mouth opening.

Put on your beard, cape and hat to become a fantastical wizard. If you want a wand to cast spells, follow the instructions on pages 16 and 17, but ask a grown-up to spray paint it silver instead of using the fairy design shown there.

Monster party

By using some card, layers of newspaper and other things often found around the house, you can make these monstrous hands and face.

YOU WILL NEED:

strong card, pencil, scissors, thin card, black pen, PVA glue, kitchen sponge, drinking straw, tape, newspaper or an old telephone directory, wallpaper paste, string, paint, paintbrush, four bolts, wool, thin elastic, dowel stick or garden cane, jumper

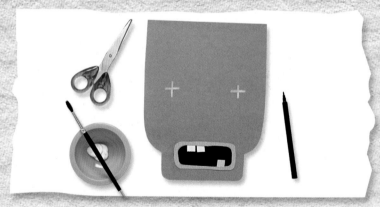

STEP 1

Copy the shape of the mask shown above onto a piece of strong card that is 20 centimetres high and 16 centimetres wide. Make crosses for the eyes. Cut out the mask, then cut out the eyes.

STEP 2

Cut a pair of squarish lips from thin card. Place them on the mask, draw around them and remove the lips. Colour the area inside the line with a black pen. Snip three teeth from white card. Glue the top of each tooth behind the lips. Glue the lips to the front of the mask.

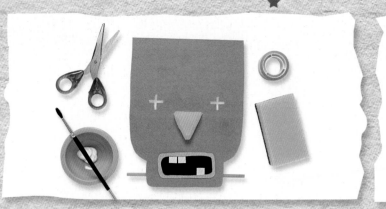

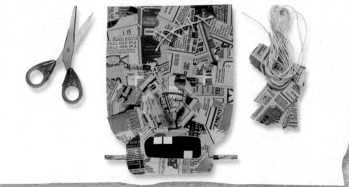

STEP 3

Snip a triangular piece of kitchen sponge to make a nose, and glue it to the mask. Cut an 18 centimetre length of drinking straw and stick it down behind the mask, using a piece of newspaper and wallpaper paste.

STEP 4

Cover the mask, and the straw ends, in newspaper and wallpaper paste. Cut a 10-centimetre long piece of string and six pieces 3 centimetres long. While the paper is wet, stick the string down on the forehead to create a gruesome scar.

STEP 5

Paint the mask bright green. You might need to use a few coats of paint. Leave each coat to dry before painting the next.

STEP 6

Slide two bolts along each painted straw end. Add a blob of glue to hold them in place.

STEP 7

Cut two 1-centimetre x 4.5-centimetre strips of black card to make eyebrows and a 6-centimetre x 17-centimetre piece to make hair. Add glue onto one side of each card, then press short pieces of black wool onto it. Once dry, snip the wool level.

Monster party

STEP 8

Glue the eyebrows onto the monster face and stick the hair behind the mask. Poke two holes at each side of the mask. Feed the ends of a piece of elastic through each hole and tie knots at the ends.

STEP 9

To make a monster hand, trace around a grown-up's hands onto card and cut them out.

STEP 10

Tape a dowel stick or piece of garden cane securely to the back of one card hand.

STEP 11

Scrunch newspaper into balls. Glue them over the back of the other hand.

STEP 12

Set the two hands together so the scrunched paper and stick are sandwiched inside. Tape together around the edges.

STEP 13

Tear more newspaper into small pieces and use wallpaper paste to stick them to the hand. Cover with a layer of newspaper.

STEP 14

Repeat steps 9 to 13 for the second hand. Cut ten fingernails from a kitchen sponge. Glue them to the end of each finger.

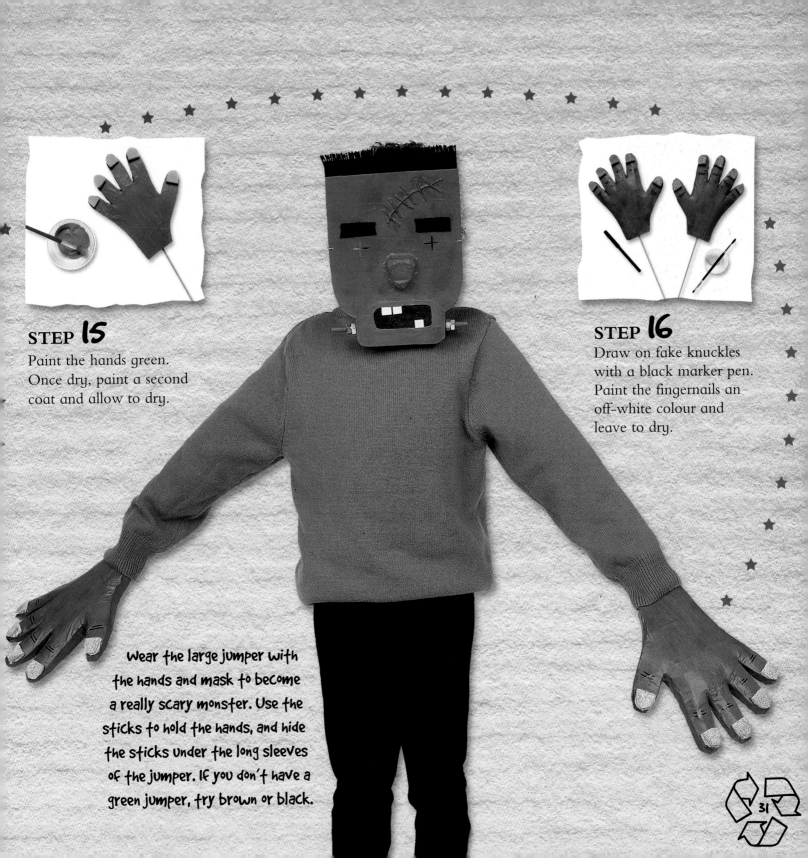

STEP 15

Paint the hands green. Once dry, paint a second coat and allow to dry.

STEP 16

Draw on fake knuckles with a black marker pen. Paint the fingernails an off-white colour and leave to dry.

Wear the large jumper with the hands and mask to become a really scary monster. Use the sticks to hold the hands, and hide the sticks under the long sleeves of the jumper. If you don't have a green jumper, try brown or black.

Skull and bones

With a pair of socks and gloves, some card and a bin liner, you can become a really frightening skeleton. Use the biggest and thickest bag you can find to make the best skeleton.

YOU WILL NEED:
....
bin liner, chalk, scissors, double-sided tape, white paint, paintbrush, old pair of gloves, pair of socks, card, pen, pencil, elastic

ECoFACT
Recycled plastic can be made into bin liners. By buying bin liners made from recycled plastic, your family will help to increase the demand for items made from recycled materials. Using recycled materials is an important step in the recycling process.

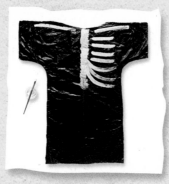

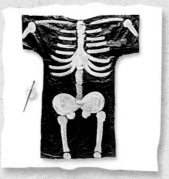

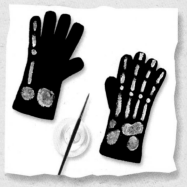

STEP 1
With chalk, draw a T-shirt shape (and neckline) onto a bin liner. Cut it out. Use double-sided tape to tape the edges together.

STEP 2
Cut an opening down the back. Start to paint a skeleton on the front by painting the spine down the centre. Add ribs and the shoulder and arm bones to it.

STEP 3
Continue painting the skeleton, adding the pelvis (hip bones) and leg bones. Leave to dry, then paint bones on the back side of the liner.

STEP 4
On a pair of gloves, paint the wrist bones at the bottom, then paint the small bones of the fingers. Allow the paint to dry.

STEP 5

Cut a piece of card about the size of your foot and slide it inside a sock. This will flatten the sock to make it easier to paint.

STEP 6

For each sock, paint the ankle bones, then the bones for each toe, and finish with the leg bones. Allow the paint to dry. (Don't forget to remove the card.)

No one will ever guess who is hiding inside this scary skeleton costume.

STEP 7

Draw a 25-centimetre x 16-centimetre skull on card, with eyes, nose and teeth as shown. Cut out the mask and eyes. Cut around the teeth and nose, leaving them attached.

STEP 8

Paint the skull white. Once dry, paint black around the mouth, nose and eyes. Poke holes in each side. Feed the ends of a piece of elastic through the holes and knot them.

Feisty fire-breather

A fire-breathing dragon will be a real match in a battle against the shining knight (see pages 40–43). You can make your costume from some plastic bags, cereal boxes and a plastic bottle.

YOU WILL NEED:
....

card, pen, scissors, paint, paintbrush, plastic bottle, PVA glue, elastic, paper, bin liner, tape, ribbon

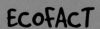

ECOFACT
The number of plastic bottles recycled in the UK since 2002 has doubled, and 727 million plastic bottles were recycled in 2004. But this is only 7.9 per cent of plastic bottles used in the home. About 9.2 billion plastic bottles are thrown away each year.

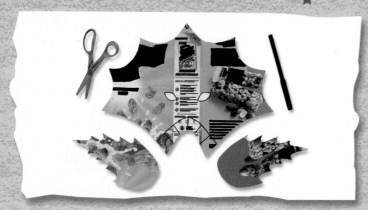

STEP 1

For the mask, using the template on page 47, trace the face and ears onto a piece of card (see page 9). Cut out the face and ears, and make sure you cut out the eyes.

STEP 2

Paint the face and ears a bright green colour. When the paint is dry, cut slits in the bottom of the mask to make flaps (these are marked on the template).

34

STEP 3

Ask a grown-up to cut the end off a large plastic bottle. Then ask the grown-up to make a pair of holes for the nostrils (the flames will fit into these) as well as a slit to fit the tongue in.

STEP 4

Paint the bottle green to match the mask and leave to dry. Paint in the white teeth, and outline the teeth with gold paint. Add a decorative gold edge around the mouth and black around the nostrils.

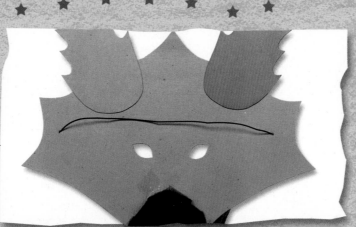

STEP 5

When the paint is dry, glue the ears to the top of the mask, sticking them to the back of the mask. Allow the glue to dry.

STEP 6

Poke a hole at each end of the mask. Cut a piece of elastic that will fit around your head when attached to the mask. Feed one end into a hole and make a knot in the end. Feed the other end into the second hole, test the fit and tie a knot. Cut off the extra elastic.

STEP 7

Place the bottle over the bottom of the mask and fold the tabs into it. Glue the tabs to the bottle and leave it to dry.

Feisty fire-breather

STEP 8

Cut pieces of yellow and red paper to make flames, and also cut a piece of red paper to make a forked tongue. Glue these into the slits in the bottle. Finish the mask by painting some decorative lines using gold paint.

STEP 9

For the wings, cut open a large bin liner, cutting down one side and along the bottom. Unfold the liner so you can find the top edge of the wings — use a long edge of the rectangle as the top.

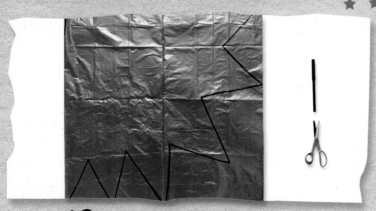

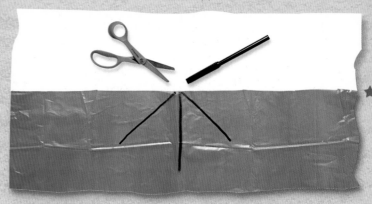

STEP 10

Fold the liner in half from side to side, then draw a border of triangular shapes with a pen along two unfolded edges. Cut out the border. Unfold the liner.

STEP 11

Make a neck opening at the centre of the straight top edge by drawing three lines 10 centimetres long, with the middle one straight down, and the two outer ones at 45 degree angles, as shown. Cut slits along the lines. Paint on scales and lines with gold paint. Leave to dry.

STEP 12

Cut a length of ribbon long enough to fit around your neck and tie a bow. Place it centred at the neck opening, fold the tabs over it and glue them down.

STEP 13

Cut some elastic to fit around your wrist and fold it into a loop. Tape it to the top point on one side of the wings. Repeat for the other side.

To wear your wings, tie the ribbon around your neck and slide your wrists through the loops. When your mask is hiding your face, who wouldn't be scared of such a ferocious fire-breathing dragon?

A shining knight

You can make your very own sword, tabard, shield and helmet to become a knight in shining armour. You'll be ready to fight off dragons as you rescue damsels in distress.

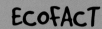

YOU WILL NEED:

felt (use two different colours), ruler, black pen, pair of compasses, scissors, PVA glue, paintbrush, tracing paper, pencil, corrugated card, paint, aluminium foil, two paper fasteners, hat elastic

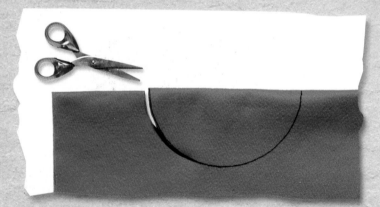

STEP 1

To make the tabard, fold a piece of 150-centimetre x 40-centimetre felt in half, with the short edges together. For the neck opening, draw a 19-centimetre-diameter semi-circle on the fold and cut it out.

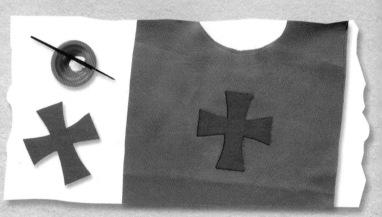

STEP 2

Follow the design shown here to draw a 16-centimetre cross onto a piece of red felt – make the bottom part of the cross a little longer than the side and top parts. Cut out the cross. Glue the cross to the front of the tabard.

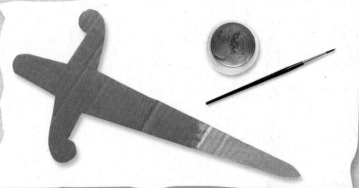

STEP 3

Draw a 40-centimetre long sword shape, as shown here, onto paper and cut it out. Draw two swords onto corrugated card, using the paper sword as a guide. Ask an adult to help you cut out the two swords. Glue the swords together and leave to dry.

STEP 4

Paint one side of the sword silver. Leave it to dry, then paint the other side silver, too. (If you want, you can paint the handle a different colour.)

STEP 5

Draw the shape of the 33-centimetre x 38-centimetre shield shown here onto corrugated card. Ask an adult to cut it out. Cut a shield from aluminium foil the same size as the card, but add 2.5 centimetres to the edges. Place the card shield onto the foil. Fold over the edges of the foil and glue to the card.

STEP 6

Cut another shield from foil the same size as the cardboard shield, but trim about 5 millimetres from the edges. Glue the foil to the back of the card shield.

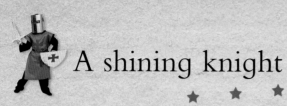

A shining knight

STEP 7

Cut a second cross from red felt (see step 2). Glue the cross to the front of the shield. Allow the glue to dry.

STEP 8

For a handle, ask an adult to cut a 20-centimetre x 4-centimetre strip of corrugated card, cutting the short edges parallel with the lines of the card. Bend the handle between your fingers to curve it.

STEP 9

Ask an adult to poke a pair of holes in the shield and handle. Insert a paper fastener through the holes on the shield, then the holes on the handle. Open the prongs.

STEP 10

Cut a visor from card, making it a 21-centimetre x 44-centimetre rectangle. With a long side at top, cut out the eye holes about 7 centimetres from the top and 4 centimetres apart. Paint the visor silver. Leave to dry.

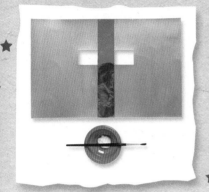

STEP 11

Cut a 22.5-centimetre x 4-centimetre strip of foil. Glue the strip to the visor, folding the ends over to the back side of the visor.

STEP 12

Ask an adult to poke a hole at each side of the visor. Feed elastic through the holes and make knots in the ends.

Put on your tabard and helmet and grab your shield and sword to turn yourself into a brave knight.

Shiver me timbers!

Everything a pirate needs is included in this costume: a stripy shirt, bandana, cutlass, pirate's hat, eye patch and even a telescope. All you'll need is a parrot!

YOU WILL NEED:
....
old white (or light-coloured) T-shirt, scissors, paint, paintbrush, red fabric, paper, pencil, ruler or tape measure, card, pen, PVA glue, tape, elastic, cardboard tubes

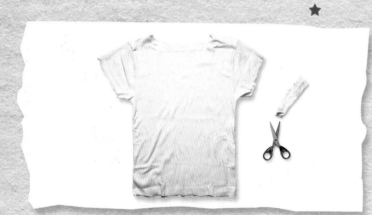

STEP 1
To make your shirt look really rugged, cut off the ends of the sleeves, cut off the bottom of the shirt and cut off the neckline.

STEP 2
Paint blue stripes across the shirt and around the sleeves. Allow the paint to dry, then paint stripes across the back of the shirt, too.

STEP 3

To make a bandana, cut a piece of red fabric into a 45-centimetre square. Fold the square into a triangular shape.

STEP 4

Draw a cutlass shape, as shown above, onto paper, with the blade 45 centimetres long and the handle 15 centimetres long. Cut it out and use it to draw two cutlass shapes onto card, facing opposite directions. Cut them out and glue together.

STEP 5

Cut an oval from a piece of card to make a hand protector. Make a slit in it to slip over the cutlass handle and glue in place.

STEP 6

Now use the paper cutlass to draw and make two more handle shapes. Cut these out and glue one to each side of the handle.

STEP 7

Paint one side of the blade silver and one side of the handle black. Once dry, paint the other sides.

43

Shiver me timbers!

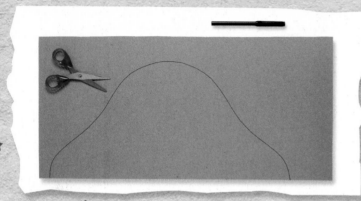

STEP 8

Draw a pirate's hat shape onto a piece of paper and cut it out. (Measure your head beforehand to get an idea of how large to make it.) Use this to trace two pirate hat shapes onto card, then cut them out.

STEP 9

Stick pieces of sticky tape along the top edge of the two hat shapes to hold them together.

STEP 10

Paint the hat black. Once dry, paint a white skull and crossbones on the front of the hat.

STEP 11

Cut a band of card to fit your head. Tape the ends, then tape it inside the hat.

STEP 12

Draw the shape of an eye patch onto a piece of card, as shown here. Cut it out.

STEP 13

Paint the eye patch black and leave to dry. (Don't paint the side that will be facing your eye.)

STEP 14

Poke two holes into the eye patch. Feed the ends of a length of elastic into them, and knot the ends.

STEP 15

To make a telescope, cut a slit partway down one end of a long cardboard tube. Cut a shorter piece from another tube.

STEP 16

Paint the tubes black with a silver band. Once dry, slip the short tube over the long tube over the slit (don't paint this end silver).

When you want to be a treasure-hunting pirate, put on your shirt, tie the bandana around your neck and use a wide belt to hold either your cutlass or your telescope.

Cat template

(for pages 24–25)

This template has been reduced to half the size so it will fit on this page. You'll need to enlarge it by 200% on a photocopier that has A3 paper. Trace along the dotted line separately to make the muzzle of the cat.

Dragon template
(for pages 34–35)

This template has been
reduced to half the size
so it will fit on this page.
You'll need to enlarge
it by 200% on a
photocopier that
has A3 paper.

Index

Special thanks to our models:
Jessica, Joseph, Oliver,
Pia and Safia (and thanks
to their mums and dads, too).

48